Pandaw

Pandaw

The Irrawaddy Flotilla Company and
the Rivers of Myanmar

Paul Strachan

KISCADALE PUBLICATIONS

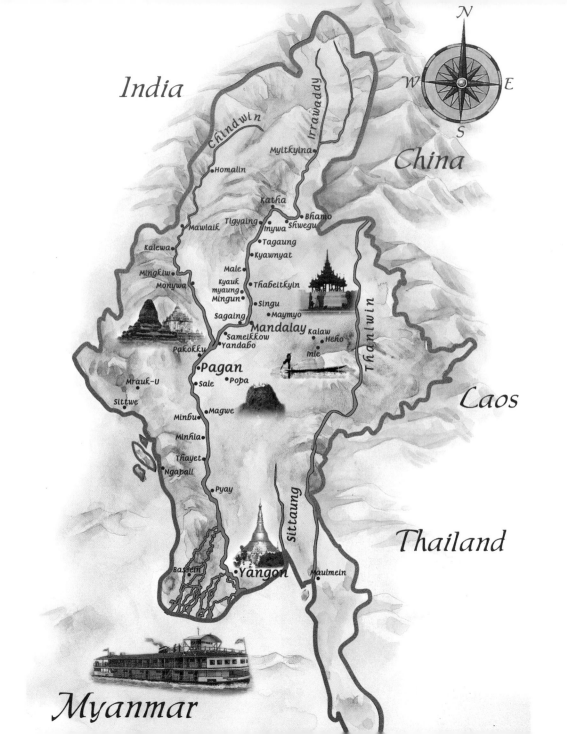

India

Chindwin

Irrawaddy

China

Myitkyina

Homalin

Katha

Tigyaing   Bhamo
Mawlaik   Inywa Shwegu
                Tagaung
Kalewa   Kyawnyat
                Male
Mingkiw   Kyauk
Monywa   myaung   Thabeitkyin
              Mingun
              Sagaing   Singu
                        Maymyo
              Samelkkow Mandalay Kalaw
Pakokku   Yandabo   Heho
                                  Inle
              Pagan
Mrauk-U   Sale   Popa
Sittwe
              Minbu Magwe
              Minhla

              Thayet
Ngapali
              Pyay

Bassein   Yangon   Maulmein

Caos

Thaliwin

Sittaung

Thailand

Myanmar

N
W   E
S

Contents

Introduction

In 1995 when my wife Roser and I started adventure cruises on the Irrawaddy we had no idea what we were getting into. Myanmar (Burma) is a country that moves: whether by the vastness of its panoramas, its vibrant river landscapes, or by the intellectual and artistic wealth of two millennia of Buddhist culture. But above all, one can not help be moved by the warmth, friendliness and welcome of the Myanma people.

I had been fascinated by Mynamar since my first long stay in 1981 and had become a keen student of Myanmar art and history. In the early 90s I built up a small publishing business producing academic and art books on Myanmar. Through this I was able to maintain regular contact with the country. On such a visit to Yangon in 1995 I found a locally-made ship and decided to charter it for an exploratory cruise to Bhamo. The idea was to invite as many of the readers of our books to share the charter cost. Before we knew it we were booked out. And then we had to run a further six trips that season.

Being the first people to offer river cruises since the days of the old Irrawaddy Flotilla, we rather cheekily copied the name of that once great Scots company. The ship we chartered was of doubtful construction and with each day a new set of crises unfolded. We never reached Bhamo, but learnt an awful lot about the river. The next year we found a slightly better ship and ran her until in 1997 we discovered the original *Pandaw*, an old colonial-style river steamer from the 1940s built on the Clyde.

It is nearly a decade since we revived the Irrawaddy Flotilla Company and we run the original *Pandaw* and two identical, though enlarged, replicas of this historic ship that we have built from scratch. It is a proud boast that we now offer some of the highest standards of comfort and service to be found in Myanmar.

This, combined with an expeditionary atmosphere and the character and charm of a colonial ship, makes us unique and the best choice for exploring the real Myanmar. With a European management team of five professionals and a local staff of over 100 we are completely dedicated to the care of our passengers. We have grown to be the largest upmarket river cruising company in Myanmar and are presently expanding into other rivers in other countries.

All our team are committed to an ethical and environmentally friendly form of tourism. We have strict guidelines for our passengers when visiting remote areas and firmly believe that the benefits of a thoughtful and sensitive tourism far outweigh any negative impact. We are a completely private company in Myanmar using locally owned services and people and, wherever possible, supporting the local economy.

Our passengers have become involved in a number of projects to assist the development of the local communities who welcome us so warmly. The Pandaw School catering for 500 children is now complete at Yandabo and this year a second one will be finished at Thein Gone near Pakokku.

If you have not yet been, I very much hope that you will come to Myanmar to see these vast rivers so full of human activity for yourself. You will find, as we have, that the Pandaws the most tranquil yet practical way of seeing the real Myanmar in great style and comfort.

Paul Strachan

The Old Flotilla

The original Irrawaddy Flotilla was a naval task force of paddle steamers and flats (barges) sent from India to transport British and Indian troops up river in the Second Anglo-Burmese War of 1852. Unlike the First War, when the British were caught out by the monsoon, this war was a highly organised affair. Preparations in India were extensive and included the transfer of steam paddle ships of the Bengal Marine for troop transportation on the Irrawaddy. These were officered by British and crewed by lascars. Taking advantage of divisions at the Court of Ava, the flotilla advanced rapidly up the river capturing Prome and then the prized Myédé forests just above Thayetmyo. The British had never intended to hack off so large a chunk of territory, the original plan was to capture and hold Martaban, Rangoon and Bassein – the important southern ports. The Province of Pegu, rendered defenceless by a government in turmoil, with its extensive forests and rich resources was too great a spoil. Interestingly the commander of the naval operations, who died of illness on the river, was the brother of the author Jane Austen, Rear-Admiral Austen. Meanwhile, at the capital of Amarapura the king, Pagan Min, was deposed by Mindon who promptly negotiated a treaty with the British.

In 1864 the Governor of British Myanmar, Sir Arthur Phayre decided to privatise the flotilla. After the cessation of hostilities it had been assigned to peace time duties. Todd, Findlay & Co, a Scots firm established originally in Moulmein and latterly in the emerging capital of Rangoon, purchased the four steamers and three flats. As a sweetener the government guaranteed mail contracts, but, given the poor condition of the vessels, Todd, Findlay& Co. had nothing but trouble with them.

The potential had been realised, and in 1865 a company was formed in Glasgow with the shipping line Paddy Hendersons, who were already established in Myanmar with Rangoon a port of call on their New Zealand runs, and Denny's of Dunbarton, the shipbuilders. This partnership of merchants, shippers and ship builders was to offer a combined expertise and experience that gave the company an entrepreneurial thrust linked to a grasp of technology.

By the late 1860s it proved necessary to replace the old government steamers and new vessels were built on the Clyde, dismantled and shipped out for reconstruction in Rangoon. It took some years and much trial and error before the company perfected a design suited to the difficult conditions of the Irrawaddy with its perilous shallows. By 1872 the fleet comprised eight new steamers and twelve flats. Services operated between Rangoon and Prome in British Myanmar, in Royal Myanmar up to Mandalay, and by 1869 to Bhamo.

The company had early realised the importance of the China trade and saw the importance of a river link to South West China through Myanmar. Though King Mindon was said to have moved capital to Mandalay from Ava in 1855 out of irritation at the sound of passing steamer's whistles, and despite efforts to establish a flotilla of his own, the company prospered in Royal Myanmar thanks to the close relationship between the company agent, Dr Clement Williams, and the king.

In 1885 the flotilla was used in the 3rd Anglo Burmese War to

THE IRRAWADDY CAPTAIN...

"Some of the steamers that come this way are of the largest size; mailers on their way from Mandalay; cargo boats with flats in tow, laden with produce of the land; and when they come round the bend into full view of Maubin, the great stream shrinks and looks strangely small, as if it were being overcome by a monster from another world. Three hundred feet they are in length, these steamers with flats in tow, half as wide, and they forge imperiously ahead as if all space belonged to them, and swing round and roar out their anchor chains, while the lascars leap and the skipper's white face gleams in the heavy shadows by the wheel – the face of a man in command."

SCOTT O'CONNER, *THE SILKEN EAST*, 1936

Above: Steamer with flats moored at Mandalay
Below: Delta class steamer

STRANGE CARGOS

" – *great bales of cotton, bags of rice, blocks of jade, lacquerware from Pagan, silk, tamarind, elephants sometimes, woven mats, maize, jaggery, bullocks, marble Buddhas, oilcake, tobacco, timber. Upward bound will be found various imports from Europe, motor cars, corrugated iron, condensed milk, matches, aluminium ware, sewing machines, piece goods, soap, cigarettes, cement and whisky. Every class of goods that enters or leaves Myanmar finds its way onto an Irrawaddy boat.*"

IRRAWADDY FLOTILLA COMPANY HANDBOOK, 1936

Left: a T-class ferry built in the late 40s plies between Pagan and Prome, 1999
Above: 1st class passengers take tiffin on an old IFC express steaemer, c.1900

transport an entire army into Royal Myanmar to occupy Mandalay with scarcely a shot fired. For the following sixty years till the Japanese invasion of 1942 the story of Myanmar, with her rise to great wealth and economic supremacy amongst the Asian nations, is intertwined with the operations and activities of the Irrawaddy Flotilla Company. Scots guile was quick to realise that Myanmar was a land of rivers and even with the completion of roads and railways the river remained the key to the riches of Myanmar.

By the 1920s the fleet consisted of 622 units (267 powered) from the magnificent Siam class of 326 feet long (the same length as the height of the Shwedagon) and licenced to carry 4,000 passengers to pilot craft and tug boats. In a normal year the company carried eight million passengers (without loss of life) and 1.25 million tons of cargo. Irrawaddy vessels tended to have side paddles and would tow two flats, each lashed to either side.

On the Chindwin, which was pioneered during Thibaw's reign by company steam launch in 1875, a radical new design was created by Denny's to cope with the shallow conditions. To balance the displacement the paddle was situated in the stern and the boiler in the bow. This sternwheeler type would draw only 2.5 feet of water and as the Chindwin valley was wooded regular fueling stations were set up so a vessel did not need to burden itself.

The larger company ships had Scots masters and engineers and lascar crews recruited mainly from the Chittagong area, the lesser ones were entirely Chittagonian. The company had 200 mainly Scots expats based in Myanmar and a local staff of 11,000. Head

WITH LORD DUFFERIN IN BURMA—THE ADVANCE GUARD ON BOARD THE "SIR WILLIAM PEEL"—"NO DACOITS YET"
FROM A SKETCH BY OUR SPECIAL ARTIST, MR. F. VILLIERS

office was in Glasgow but in those pleasant phoneless and faxless days regional 'Assistants' were autonomous. There was one telegram a month from Rangoon to Glasgow and that consisted of one line only – the takings!

In addition to passenger and cargo transport the company operated a fleet of oil barges to carry crude oil from the Chauk area to the Syriam oil refinery for the Myanmarh Oil Company. Paddy was carried for Steel Brothers on specially designed paddy boats and timber for the Bombay Burmah Company. All these commercial undertakings were Scots.

In 1934 the Irrawaddy Flotilla & Airways was set up offering scheduled services and charters – including an unusual service for devout Buddhists whereby an aircraft would encircle the Magwe pagoda seven times.

The passing of company steamers was part of river life and when the company changed steamer design and removed a funnel there was an outcry amongst the Burmese villagers. A 2nd, dummy funnel had to be added in the interests of public relations.

The story of the Irrawaddy Flotilla is a story of Scottish-Burmese partnership. Two dissimilar nations established a rapport and shared a prodigious wealth that neither country had known before or since. The demise of the flotilla was perhaps the saddest day of British merchant marine histor. When else have six hundred ships been lost in one fell swoop? In 1942, before the oncoming Imperial Japanese Army, the company's own officers gunned holes in the great ships hulls rather than let them fall into enemy hands. It was called an 'Act of Denial'.

Above: the Rangoon River port, c.1880s
Below: the ghats at Pagan, 1886, with royal ships sunk in the 3rd Anglo-Burmese War

Rivers of Myanmar

Myanmar is a former British colony that in 1962 closed its doors to the world. Isolated, the culture and way of life of this devoutly Buddhist country escaped the changes that affected her South-East Asian neighbours. Today, along the banks of her great rivers, life continues undisturbed by the worst excesses of the modern world. Here is a rich and vibrant culture, supported by a healthy domestic economy, and populated by an overpoweringly friendly people. Even the most travelled of travellers find themselves in a world that is beyond both experience and imagining.

The Irrawaddy gives Myanmar its life. Named after the Hindu eravati or 'elephant river' the river in Burmese consciousness, like the Ganges to the Indian, is a sacred entity; provider of the wherewithal for life and happiness; material and spiritual well being.

Rising in the southern Himalayas, the Irrawaddy dissects the land from north to south for 1,350 miles, emptying through a nine-armed delta into the Indian Ocean. In colonial times, before railways and car roads the river was known as the 'Road to Mandalay'.

There are few rivers so scenically diverse as the Irrawaddy. From the three dramatic gorges north of Mandalay, where the river narrows as it passes through forested mountains and jungles, to vast plains where in the Hot Season the river breaks up into myriad channels and streams separated by sandbars and gleaming white islands. In places the river can be several miles wide and just to cross from one bank to another can be a day's sail, zig zagging through the maze of dune covered humps. Yet when it rains, the water level can rise a hundred feet drowning such archipelagae of silt and sand and washing it away in a brown torrent at speeds of up to ten miles an hour. Desert becomes ocean, and the fishermen and cultivators who have camped on these fertile islands are up and gone for the duration of the monsoon.

The Irrawaddy was and is the home of Myanmar's rich Buddhist civilisation – the ancient Pyu cities, the first empire of Pagan and later empire of Ava, all straddled the banks of the great river. Mandalay the last royal capital of Myanmar, remains the largest upstream port with literally thousands of vessels, from traditional rice barges and sampans to Clyde-built line steamers all moored in one great tangle along her ghats. As with the Nile in Egypt, Myanmar history and culture is rooted along the river's banks and a river cruise is the most practical way of seeing the land, from ancient cities to jungle villages.

The Chindwin joins the Irrawaddy just above Pagan, and though a tributary, it too is one of the great rivers of Asia. The Chindwin is even more treacherous to navigate than the Irrawaddy. Rising in the wet hills of Assam, the Upper Chindwin dissects successive mountain ranges to divulge its vast cargo of melten snow into the aptly named Dry Zone of Upper Myanmar. The Lower Chindwin can be miles wide, yet with an average dry season depth of only three feet.

The Irrawaddy and Chindwin are of interest not just for their moving natural beauty, but because along these are the arteries through which the livelihood of Myanmar flows. Gazing out from the Pandaw's promenades and extensive observation decks there is never a dull moment on the Irrawaddy. From watching fishermen working their nets from tiny canoes, to following the progress of log rafts the size of football pitches, complete with hut encampments, there is always something happening as we drift by.

Whole families live on the river where they find a living. From

The Chindwin near Kalewa

humble fisher folk to rich merchantmen speculating as they move produce from port to port. Villages of rafters in the employ of the timber enterprises make, with their families, cats, dogs, chickens and all, an annual peregrination from the northern forests to the delta plains. Gold panners form floating Klondikes: water-borne villages of hundreds of boats tethered together midstream, bound by a common hope of finding wealth in the passing tons of mud and silt. Whether collecting drift wood to sell as tinder, salvaging scuppered hulks from the war, or gypsy scavengers and even pirates, human activity on the river is incessant .

The Irrawaddy is an untamable river – there are neither locks nor weirs to control the level as on the Missisipi or Nile – and in the monsoon the water level has an average rise 50 feet and in places like the First Defile there is a rise of 200 feet. The river is thus exceptionally difficult to navigate - no two journeys are ever the same. In the low water season channels block and long diversions are required. In the wet season the flow can be so strong that a powerful vessel can stand still against the current.

On the Irrawaddy there are no charts, for the sands shift with such rapidity that they would be out of date before the ink is dry. Instead, the company operated its fleet safely and efficiently through the experience of her masters and pilots and a clever and inexpensive system of bamboo marker buoys. Buoy Boats in charge of beats constantly checked and marked the channels with buoys and the bearings with marker posts on the river banks. If a captain went aground he had to stay with his vessel, in the case of the Momein in 1919 for a whole year. In 1877 the Kha Byoo was caught in a whirlpool in the second defile between Katha and Bhamo. She spent three days spinning in a circle before getting free and the captain's hair turned white. In the old days a number of river features were named after incidents they experienced at their hands, thus there was 'Becketts's Bluff' or' MacFarlane's Folly'.

The Irrawaddy near Katha, sail-powered craft are a common sight, particularly in the Monsoon and period just after

17

both people and elephants bathe at least twice a day in the fast flowing rivers; on the left is a floating village of gold sifters on the Chindwin

Fishing on the Upper Chindwin in the swollen brown waters of the late Monsoon

Early morning on the Irrawaddy, near Sameikkon

The Pandaw Story

Ajourney on the Irrawaddy River is one of life's great travel experiences. No vessel could be more appropriate for this than a ship of the Pandaw Fleet.

Built in Scotland in 1947, the *Pandaw* is the same design as the original shallow draft Irrawaddy Flotilla Company paddle steamers that coped so well with the difficult conditions of the Irrawaddy.

In 1997 we discovered old Pandaw laid-up at Mandalay. It was love at first sight. But her condition was terrible. On account of her ultra shallow draft she had been used mainly on the Mandalay-Bhamo run. Often passing through insurgent controlled areas she would be fired upon so her sides and wheel house had been plated-up for protection. (On one occasion a sister P class ship in the 2nd Defile was mortared by insurgents and sank.) Pigs ran freely on the lower deck and fifty years of overloading with passengers and goods had taken its toll. Yet Yarrows build a strong ship and we reckoned she was good for another fifty years. Sir Eric Yarrow came out for the re-launch in 1998 and made it clear to all that the guarantee had expired.

The *Pandaw* and her six sisters had been ordered from Yarrows by the Inland Water Transport Board, the successor to the IFC, who were nationalised in 1948 immediately upon Independence. They were stern wheelers and intended to replace the 'fabulous flotilla', as the IFC fleet was known that had been sunk in the war. Built in a pre-war colonial-style, the design continued the old IFC tradition of shallow draft technology and open decks for the particular conditions of Upper Myanmar. These vessels were all sailed out from Glasgow, boarded up for the sea passage. The class is called P because all their names begin with a *p* like Pandaw.

When we went on board in 1997 there was an old sailor who could remember her in the early 50s – he recalled the fine brass work and elegant fittings, long since stripped away and sold off.

The stern paddles were removed and replaced with diesel-driven outboard rudder-propellers in the 1970s.

We acquired her from Inland Water Transport and spent a year re-fitting her. We tried to conserve as many original features as we could, restoring her to recreate the atmosphere and character of the first class deck of a colonial river steamer. Using old photos and models and interviewing a number of the old company's former employees the restoration was as authentic as was possible. Being in Myanmar advantage was made of beautiful local hardwoods, such as teak, and excellent local craftsmanship. The Pandaw was re-launched in September 1998 with the addition of sixteen luxurious staterooms, described in the Lonely Planet Guide a "a teak and brass Raj-era fantasy". The World Ship Trust have included Pandaw in the *International Register of Historic Ships*.

We will never forget how one day walking in that most delightful yet remote of towns, Katha, an old lady asked me how we had got there. We replied that we had come on the Pandaw, her response: "oh, so have they repaired her at last".

The *Pandaw* became popular. Demand exceeded all expectations. For this reason the company decided to introduce a second vessel into service for November 2001. *Pandaw II* is of similar design to the original Pandaw but slightly larger. We built her new in a Rangoon dockyard to our own exacting standards with very clear ideas of how a river cruise ship in the tropics should work best for passengers and crew.. The much loved and generously sized staterooms of *Pandaw I* were faithfully reproduced as has the character and atmosphere of a colonial river steamer.

Following the success of *Pandaw II*, the first passenger cruise ship ever to be built in Myanmar, an even larger *Pandaw III* was launched in November 2002 with further improvements to design and efficiency, without sacrifice to charm and authenticity.

မြည်တွင်းရေကြောင်းသယ်ယူပို့ဆောင်ရေးအဖွဲ့
(ရေဝတီဌာန)

Above: Pamdaw I at Khan-nyat; below left: a P class ship, boarded up for passage to Myanmar, undergoing trials on the Clyde; below right: a P class vessel in operation in the late 40s - the flying bridge was added after arrival in Myanmar

Above: Pandaw I at nightfall; opposite top: a rare photo taken by Tony Wheeler of a P class ship in 1979, then still under paddle power; passengers go ashore at Yandabo observed from the bridge

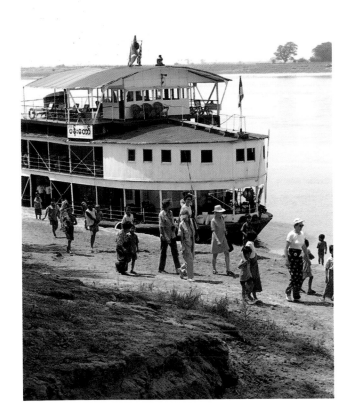

The shipyard in Rangoon with Pandaw II and III under construction

On Board a Pandaw

All our ships follow a similar layout and design with staterooms on two decks opening onto circumambulatory promenades furnished with rattan reading chairs. The key ingredient to the success of the Pandaw design has been the fact that we offer our passengers copious amounts of fresh air. Unlike other ships we are not cooped up all day in a steel box with hermetically sealed windows. On the Pandaw windows open; walls slide back and all but disappear. Ventilation is natural, not ducted. We are close at all times to a real river world that is unfolding all about us.

On each Pandaw there is an observation or sun deck above. This is part covered by an awning and offers a bar service with complimentary coffee and tea ready on the side board from dawn to dusk. Here you will find the bridge and with our open bridge policy you can follow the fascinating work of the ship's officers and pilots as they ply seemingly invisible channels with neither charts nor modern navigational aids.

Local materials like rattan and home-spun fabrics are used in the furnishing and decoration of the ship. Thoughtful detail in all aspects of the design remembering that this is a ship, not a hotel, and space is precious.

The ships have teak decks and panelling throughout, inside and out, not to mention the use of other plantation hardwoods mixed to rich effect with the teak. The Pandaw Collections of paintings, old prints and objects of art make the atmosphere on board more akin to being on an elegant 1920s motor yacht than a cruise ship.

No one need be deterred from making the river trip in Myanmar by any fear as to the nature of the accommodation provided on one of its steamers. In the depths of the jungle, one thousand miles from Rangoon he can live as luxuriously as in any hotel ashore.

IRRAWADDY FLOTILLA COMPANY HANDBOOK, 1935

The Saloon, with its well stocked cocktail bar, is in the forepart of the Upper Deck and this is a favourite place for passengers to sit in the afternoons and enjoy the incoming breeze from the windows, always opened when cruising in day time. Being of Scots origin, the Pandaw Bar prides itself on one of the finest collections of single malts east of Edinburgh! Our infamous Irrawaddy Rum Sour is made with the local rum shaken with the juice of a dozen limes.

On all our ships the Dining Room is designed to open up at the sides to allow air flow during day time meals. Both Saloon and Dining Room can be closed up at night to prevent ingress of insects and are fully air-conditioned.

All the ships in our fleet are fitted with: water and sewage treatment plants; emergency communications equipment; intercoms and PA-systems; night navigation searchlight; bakery and laundry; life rafts, life jackets and other life saving equipment; fire fighting equipment with emergency pumps and generators and emergency lighting circuits. Smoking is not allowed in any of the interior areas on a Pandaw. TV, video and slide presentation facilities are available for seminars and lectures held on board

All the Pandaws have outboard propulsion systems utilising rudder-propeller technology. With adjustable height controls for the propellers, this system offers manoeuvrability in areas of shallow water offering maximum flexibility.

Opposite: the observation deck on Pandaw III.
Following: walking the decks on all the Pandaws; our ship shops feature our own collection of handicrafts and laquerware and the comfortable saloons are a place to read or write by day and enjoy good company by night

The Pandaw Fleet

PANDAW I BUILT IN SCOTLAND 1947

LENGTH	150FT / 45 M
BEAM	32FT / 9.75M
DRAFT	3FT 90CM
ENGINES	2 x 250HP DORMAN
PROPULSION	HYDROMASTER
DECKS	3: MAIN, UPPER AND OBSERVATION
CABINS	16 STATEROOMS

Captain Thet, master of Pandaw II, has spent over 40 years on the Irrawaddy and has now risen to one of the finest commands on the river

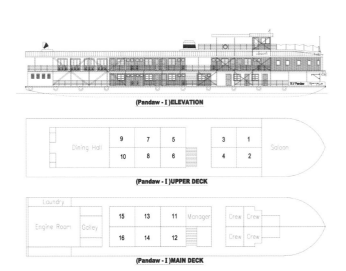

(Pandaw - I)ELEVATION

| Dining Hall | 9 | 7 | 5 | | 3 | 1 | Saloon |
| | 10 | 8 | 6 | | 4 | 2 | |

(Pandaw - I)UPPER DECK

Laundry							Crew	Crew
Engine Room	Galley	15	13	11	Manager			
		16	14	12			Crew	Crew

(Pandaw - I)MAIN DECK

PANDAW II BUILT IN YANGON IN 2001 BY IFC

LENGTH	180FT / 55M
BEAM	34FT / 10M
DRAFT	3T / 90CM
ENGINES	2 x 350HP CATERPILLARS
PROPULSION	SCHOTEL-TYPE OUTBOARD
DECKS	3: MAIN, UPPER AND OBSERVATION
CABINS	24 STATEROOMS

PANDAW III BUILT IN YANGON IN 2002 BY IFC

LENGTH	180FT / 55M
BEAM	34FT / 10M
DRAFT	3T / 90CM
DECKS	4: LOWER, MAIN, UPPER AND OBSERVATION
ENGINES	2 x 400HP CUMMINS ENGINES
PROPULSION	SCHOTEL-TYPE OUTBOARD
CABINS	28 DOUBLE STATEROOMS & 11 SINGLE CABINS

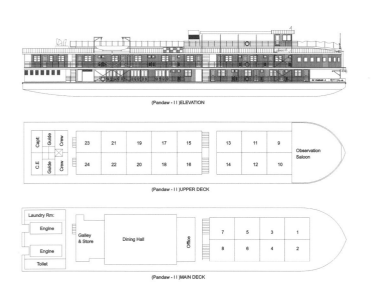

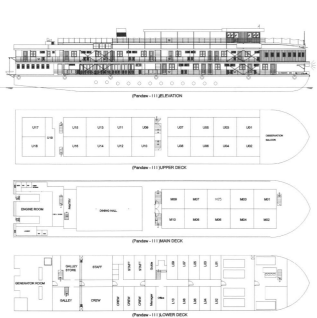

Pandaw Cruising

All our Pandaws are loved by all who sail on them... For some of our passengers it is the spacious teak-panelled staterooms, decent sized bathrooms and old world yacht feel of their accommodation. For others it is the open promenades that run around the ship that form an extension of the cabin space: the fact that on a Pandaw you are close to the river world around not hermetically sealed up like in other ships.

The average Pandaw stateroom size (170 sq ft) is considerably larger than the average on other cruise ships. Per passenger there is a greater area of public space than on any other cruise ship in the world!

Fine dining and excellent service, a hospitable caring management team all help to to make a Pandaw experience something very special. The staff to guest ratio is higher than on most other ships or hotels ensuring high levels of service and care.

There are no hidden extras on a Pandaw cruise like additional charges for unscheduled sightseeing trips; complimentary coffee and tea are available all day on the sundeck; mineral water is not charged for. Only drinks at bar and personal laundry are billed to the passenger's account.

Pandaw Cruising is not like other forms of cruising. There are no deck quoits or formal dinners at the Captain's Table. The use of the ship's Tannoy is discouraged unless in emergencies or for key announcements. A number of our passengers are artists and writers seeking the silence of the great river. Others are people with active lives in business or public affairs seeking to escape into another dimension or they are retired from such lives enjoying the tranquillity of the river in the comfort of a Pandaw .

Nothing on a Pandaw is compulsory. Passengers are welcome to join our escorted shore excursions, do their own thing, or just stay on board. On our longer cruises we organise briefings, slide shows and video presentations. When in Mandalay we arrange classical ballet performances on our sundeck that transforms into a theatre. In Pagan the famous Zawgyi-pyan marionette theatre comes on board.

Though there is ample private space for those who seek silence, a Pandaw cruise can also be a convivial experience with a group of interesting like-minded travellers exploring a little known country in the charming and historic atmosphere of a Pandaw.

Cruising on a Pandaw can be a peaceful experience interrupted only by stimulating and exciting trips ashore. Scheduled for at least once, if not twice, a day there are excursions into timeless villages and small towns. The river world we explore is remote and far from the trodden tourist track. Our shallow draft ships can ply and moor virtually anywhere on the inland waters of Myanmar thus offering penetrating insights into areas of the country that could not be reached by land.

By the old Moulmein Pagoda, lookin lazily at the sea,
There s a Myanmar girl a-settin , and I know she thinks o me;
For the wind is in the palm trees, and the temple bells they say:
'Come you back you British soldier; come you back to Mandalay'

Come you back to Mandalay,
Where the old Flotilla lay:
Can t you ear their paddles chunkin from Rangoon to Mandalay
Where the flyin fishes play,
An the dawn comes up like thunder outer China crost the Bay

RUDYARD KIPLING (1865-1936)

Log rafts are a common sight on the upper rivers after the Monsoon when the waters are still high - some rafts can be over 200ft long and have small villages constructed on them - in former times the raftsmen and their families returned the 1,000 odd miles home by canoe - now they are given bus tickets

*Pandaw II on the Bhamo expedition run: life goes on despite the intrusion of
a Pandaw and its complement of foreign travelers*

Pandaw III: at the helm or rather the electronic controls of our modern rudder-propeller system that copes so well with shallow waters

Pandaw Dining

Under the direction of our European executive chefs we have evolved a fusion cuisine combining the best of Asian and Western traditions.

We are anxious to source as much produce locally, not just to assist the economies of the areas we visit but because we know that our passengers have come to Myanmar to taste and sample local products. We offer as much tropical fruit and vegetables as we can and the fresh river fish is a favourite.

At each meal we offer a choice of spicy Asian, European, vegetarian. With advance warning special diets may be catered for. Breakfasts and lunches are simple buffets. Dinner is a sit down table d'hotê. Dress at night is smart-casual and never formal. There is a choice of table sizes - small tables for couples who want to be alone and larger ones for groups who want to be all together. There is no compulsory seating plan like on some cruise liners.

A choice of European and New World wines are available from the Pandaw cellars, or rather holds. In the cooler months the sides of the Pandaw Dining Room fold open to let the river breeze ventilate. At night we close up the sides and have air conditioning.

DINNER

Duck Terrine with Lime Coriander Dressing
***
Thick Carrot Soup
***
Oven Baked Irrawaddy Butterfish
with a Lime & Caper Sauce

Fried Tamarind River Prawn Curry
Ginger Salad and Balachaung

Market Vegetables • Mustard Seed Rice
***
Coconut Pudding • Fresh Tropical Fruits
***
Tea and Coffee • Liqueurs

Left and right: the Pandaw II dining room with lunch buffet and choice of house wines

Left: Pandaw II at breakfast time with the folding doors open bringing our passengers closer to the river world outside; above: the Pandaw III dining room and right the original Pandaw I dining room and staff

The Pandaw Stateroom

We have ensured that on all three Pandaws the much loved twin stateroom remains identical, keeping the same design features that have endeared it to so many of our past passengers. In fact, we dare not change anything!

All rooms are air conditioned with their own controls. In the Cool Season, from November to March, air conditioners are rarely required. For these times we have fitted all windows with insect screens and supply warm blankets.

There is a mini-safe in each room. Slippers and kimonos in the company livery are supplied as are mineral water, note books, pencils, etc. The bathrooms, for a ship, are very roomy with granite basin tops and smart teak loo seats. Hot water is copious and the pressure high.

Pandaw III has an additional Lower Deck with cabins for solo travellers; smallish, yet quite cosy, these all have solid brass portholes giving to the river.

Left: the single cabins on the Lower Deck of Pandaw III are cosy and have a warm atmosphere retaining the classic Pandaw teak and brass look; above: the Pandaw II Main Deck cross passage

Pagan to Mandalay

Our classic and most popular cruise provides a key link between the two principal former capitals of Myanmar – Pagan (1000-1300AD) and Mandalay (1855-1885) with their many monuments and art treasures. We sail up to four times a week in the high season and never stop overnight at either Pagan or Mandalay as there are excellent local hotels in each place. For those passengers unable to afford the time for a longer Pandaw cruise this short one or two night cruise is the perfect way to enjoy the Pandaw experience and see the river.

On each day of the cruise we stop to allow passengers to explore little known villages that are relatively unspoilt and which we work hard to keep that way. Trips ashore are led by a member of the ship's company though passengers are welcome to make their own explorations as these places are safe.

Thein Gone, situated just 10km south of Pakokku, is a charming rural village with one hundred and twenty five households.. Everyone in the village is a farmer. Thein Gone is a typical river community in which all people are cared for within the community. The Thein Gone people have asked us to assist in building a new school and monastery inland as the present buildings are threatened by river bank erosion and are flooded during the Monsoon. As Pandaw Projects concentrate on educational schemes our passengers are helping to raise funds for this.

Yandabo is a rarely visited small village with no road access to the world so it is entirely dependant on the river. It is famous for the production of pottery made from river bank mud. We see the pottery making process at various stages. We are invited into people's homes and visit the local monastery. Past Pandaw passengers have generously donated funds to build a new and modern school. Yandabo is famous in Burmese history as the place wherea treaty was signed in 1826 between the Burmese and the British.

Above: the Dhamma-yan-gyi Temple at Pagan, c.1165
Left: mural painting in the Sulamani Temple, Pagan, c.1200

Above: the Mandalay Palace, 1855
Right: the Sagaing Ponnyashin Temple, 19th century

The Golden Land

For eight years now the Irrawaddy Flotilla have offered acclaimed river expeditions to the remoter reaches of the country. The Golden Land cruise connects the Delta plain north of Yangon with the lost capitals of Pagan and Mandalay. It is by far the most culturally interesting expedition we offer.

Passing through Middle Myanmar the river is constantly changing from the vast to the narrow just as the landscape varies from jungle to forest and then near-desert. Many of the towns and villages we stop at are unconnected by roads and depend entirely on the river. Being the heartland of Myanmar the vestiges of Buddhist art and culture are rich and we visit a number of little known temples and lived-in monasteries.

As with the Nile, historic and sacred sites are situated close to the river-banks. In fact, many places we moor at cannot be reached overland. Though we have been running river expeditions for eight years, no two expeditions have ever been the same. We are constantly making new discoveries and learning more and more about these areas.

Nearly all our passengers comment that, compared with the tourist centres of Pagan and Mandalay, these river stops are far more interesting and exciting and the local people 'unspoilt'! We want to keep the river 'unspoilt' and have strict codes of conduct for our passengers to ensure that this rich and vibrant culture remains unharmed.

Our daily stops and explorations of the small riverside villages are exciting and full of interest as we interact with the local people who are ever friendly and welcoming. We visit schools and monasteries and see local agriculture and handicrafts at first hand.

We can run the Golden Land expedition year round as there are no problems with water levels in this part of Myanmar.

Left: the one mile long U Bein Bridge at Amarapura, 1841
Above: the old monastery at Sameikkon, 19th century

Upper Irrawaddy

Only possible in the high water months between May and November this expedition combines scenic interest with a study of local life and culture in remote areas of the country accessible only by water.

We start at Pagan and sail via Mandalay over 400 miles north through a lost water world. The river varies enormously: it is vast with endless winding channels just above Mandalay and then dark and narrow through the 3rd Defile. It is a constantly changing landscape with a stunning back drop of mountains.

We pass through the two dramatic defiles, jungles and forests, expanses of wetlands and vast untilled plains. Our objective is the most northerly navigable point on the river Bhamo, exactly one thousand miles from the sea. Here a small aerodrome enables us to transfer passengers back to Yangon by chartered aircraft.

Stopping at the main historic and cultural centres, we visit a number of little known small towns and villages. These form part of a vibrant river economy with thriving local industries. One of the sensations of the cruise are the 50-gallon pot workshops near Kyauk-myaung with cavernous kilns.

At Katha, once home to the writer George Orwell and setting for his novel *Burmese Days* we offer a literary tour of the colonial building's on foot. Going inland on a local bus we trek in the jungle in search of often elusive working elephants.

Bhamo until recently was off limits to foreigners. It is the ancient gateway to China and still a centre for the China trade. We go up to the border hills to visit Kachin villages and see tremendous cataracts. Though the Pandaw can go no further than Bhamo, smaller local boats can, and we hire one for a half day trip upstream to the 1st Defile with its awesome rock formations and deep gorges. At Monsoon time the water levels here can rise by 200ft.

Above: a jungle Buddha along the river side
Right: the river at Katha, once home to George Orwell

Pandaw III

Further Reading

Kiscadale Books on Myanmar

Old Yangon: City of the Shwedagon	Noel Singer	£30
Mandalay: Travels from the Golden City	Paul Strachan	£25
Myanmar: Encountering the Land of the Buddhas	Ellis Everarda	£17.99
Birmanie: (French edition of above)		£25
Myanmar: a Photographic Journey, 1855-1925	Noel F Singer	£25
Thangliena: the Life of TH Lewin	John Whitehead	£25
Inventory of Monuments at Pagan Vol.I-VI	Pierre Pichard	£85
Nat-Pwe: Myanmar's Supernatural Subculture	Yves Rodrigue	£17.95
Pagan: Art and Architecture of Old Myanmar	Paul Strachan	£25
Scots in Myanmar: Golden Times...	Alister McCrae	£14.50
South-East Asia: Languages and Literatures	P Herbert	£14.50
Myanma National Movements	U Maung Maung	£15.50
Irrawaddy Flotilla Company	Alister McCrae	ask
Paddy Henderson & Company	Dorothy Laird	ask
The Burman: His Life and Notions	Shway Yoe	£12
The Sliken East	Scott O'Connor	£12

credit card order from

www.wisdombooks.com

tel 00 44 208 5535 0200 *fax* 00 44 208 553 5122

Published in 2003 for the Irrawaddy Flotilla Company by

KISCADALE PUBLICATIONS

Text © Paul Strachan

Photographs from the Pandaw Picture Library © Irrawaddy Flotilla Compamy

by: Barry Broman, Andrea Massari, Roberto Tealdi, and Paul Strachan

ISBN 1 870838 424

Printed in Italy by Grafiche Milani

www.pandaw.com

tel 0034 972 56 10 49 *fax* 0034 972 56 10 23